101 Sizzling Tips

For Excellence on the Violin

by Sandy Hunt

Illustrated by Hallie Gillette

Published by Forest Road Productions
First Printing, July 2001

Editing and proofing by Joanna Breault, Clint Hunt
and Alexandra Hunt

Sandy dedicates this book to her dear children: Jessica, Jennifer, Joshua, Jonathan, Jordan, Justin, and Jamison, and to all those who seek to enrich their lives with music.

Published by Forest Road Productions
First Printing, July 2001

Editing and proofing by Joanna Breault, Clint Hunt and Alexandra Hunt.

Forest Road
PRODUCTIONS
PO Box 16123
Chesapeake, VA 23328

101 Table of Contents

New Music

How much should I practice?

Listen

Marking Music

Performing

Relaxed playing

START WITH GOOD HABITS

1 "GOOD HABITS ≈ BETTER PLAYING"

Practice daily.

Schedule practice sessions from Monday through Friday, leaving at least a day to rest so that your mind can refresh itself. This format will help you advance quickly while maintaining strength in your playing. Daily practice is more beneficial than practicing once a week for an extended period of time.

Keep a practice record.

A practice record will help you track daily practice times. This chart will visually show your basic practice patterns, allowing you to correct poor practice habits or confirm your feelings of accomplishment for faithful work.

Review old songs.

"How does that song go again?" Once you stop playing old tunes, you begin to lose them. Keeping a list of pieces and reviewing them will help you expand the number of selections that you can play well. You will also be able to play your earlier repertoire easier and faster. REVIEW IS SUPERB!

Practice a new piece.

Playing the same old tunes can get tiresome so we need to offer our minds a fresh new challenge. With a new song come new skills and more knowledge. Choosing and memorizing a new song is hard work. A good private teacher should keep you on the right track for learning more material. Adding new songs will broaden your performing ability.

Practice reading music.

Reading music helps to enhance and expand your skills. It takes time and effort, but once you learn how to read music you'll be able to understand any piece of music at a glance. It is wonderful to learn music quickly, not only by ear but with the added ability of note reading.

2 SETTING GOALS

Having a vision for what you are aiming for will help you align the type of training and the type of practice that you should be implementing. For example, the intermediate student might say:

"This month I will learn the two-octave G scale, study slurs, play my old songs smoother and faster, go through a music reading book that I found at the library, and memorize a new song. I could have three new songs that I can play by adding a new song each month. After dinner at 6:30 pm each day, I will practice my old songs and new songs and do exercises reading music."

3 DAILY EXERCISES FOR STRENGTH

Strength comes with exercise. Every day, place those fingers on the violin. Remember to

Pick it up! Pick it up! Pick it up!

There are many exercises that can strengthen your playing. Exercises include **bow work** using long legato bows, short chop bows, staccato bows, short, fast bows, tremolo bows, slurs, two-note slurs, four-note slurs, eight-note slurs, twelve-note slurs, etc..
Finger exercises include various finger patterns (i.e. trills, turns, grace notes and finger pops). For example, try popping your fingers down in certain patterns, such

as 1-3, 1-3, 1-3,1-4,1-4, 1-4,1-2,1-2,1-2 and so on. **Scale work** (major and minor) will help you understand the finger patterns of songs. Doing exercises that improve intonation, such as checking pitches with the open strings or practicing octaves, will help improve your ear. Practicing **Double-stops** can improve the left hand position and facilitate playing of accurate pitches. Work on **vibrato exercises** to strengthen your hand with slow-to-fast and wide-to-tight waves. Practice **improvising** and **enhance your ear** by playing along with recordings. All of these exercises will help you progress in your playing.

4   COMMITMENT AND FAITHFULNESS

Just rewards will come with diligence and time. Commit yourself to your music and learning.

Good things take time and hard work. Great performers spend many hours perfecting their music. Changing from one instrument to another, leaving each instrument behind for something else will not lead to expertise in anything. So stick with it!

You should maintain an attitude of patience, saying to yourself, *I'm in it for the long haul.* Your faithfulness will bring great rewards!

It will take many years of study to become a proficient violinist. Becoming really good at something requires a focused effort over time.

EXCELLENCE

5 TALENT CAN BE TRAINED, SO LET'S GET TO WORK!

You can be trained and molded to play music. Starting at a young age provides a great head start. Your environment needs to be a fertile one. Listening to music, practicing properly, a good teacher and a lot of work are the ingredients for successful learning!

6 THE RECIPE FOR A FINE PLAYER

Do you have what it takes to become a fine player?

2/3 cup	HEART — a passion for music!
1 full cup	STRENGTH — hard work and persistence.
3/4 cup	DILIGENCE — discipline and daily practice.
1 1/2 cup	WISDOM — an excellent teacher
	Add lots of seasoning with time and experience.

Cooking time: over a period of "years" for the best flavor!

7 STRIVE FOR EXCELLENCE IN ALL YOUR PURSUITS

You want to perform to your highest potenial. If music is your passion then put your best effort towards it. Don't settle for giving less than your best.

LUGGAGE

(LET'S MAKE SURE YOU HAVE EVERYTHING)

8   PACKING PROPERLY = PREPAREDNESS

When it is time to play, you'll want to make sure that you have everything you need. Along with your violin and bow, you will need an extra set of strings. You don't want to be incapacitated by a broken string.

CHECKLIST:

- VIOLIN AND BOW
- EXTRA STRINGS
- ROSIN
- VIOLIN CASE
- DUST RAG AND VIOLIN POLISH
- SHOULDER PAD
- METRONOME
- MUSIC STAND
- MIRROR
- TUNER
- Don't forget your copy of *101 Tips for Excellence on the Violin!*

9   INVEST IN A QUALITY VIOLIN

A cheap violin will not offer a deep, rich sound. Nicer instruments can be easier to play and keep in tune. Try out several violins and choose one that has the personality and feel that you like. A quality violin is important to your playing. Don't be in a rush to buy the first violin you see. Take your time and invest in an instrument you will play for years to come.

10 A GOOD BOW IS IMPORTANT, TOO

The bow is just as important as the instrument; it must be capable of offering the violin a good, clean, full stroke. Check for a complete set of clean bow hair. Some people invest in a nice violin but have a poor bow that can't grip the strings to pull out a tone worthy of their instrument.

Make sure that you have rosin for the bow. If the bow is running thin on horse hair, have the bow rehaired.

11 COMFORTABLE SHOULDER PAD FOR PLAYING EASE

Many performers use a shoulder pad. You will need adequate room in your case to carry it. The shoulder pad will help place the violin comfortably at the desired height. Try many different shoulder pads to find the one that best fits you. Remember, you want to be as comfortable as possible so that you will enjoy holding and practicing the violin.

12 EXTRAS FOR CONVENIENCE

An electronic tuner plays the precise "A" tuning pitch so you can tune properly. A tuner will also show whether a note is sharp or flat. Such tuners are inexpensive and beneficial particularly when a piano is not available.

Metronomes are a valuable aid for the music reader to set tempos according to the written metronomic marking.

Violin polish is nice to have to shine up the instrument before performing. A dust rag is useful for cleaning the violin of excess rosin.

A violin case with extra room for a shoulder pad, rosin, strings and other essential items is advantageous. A side pouch on the case is also convenient for carrying extra music. A shoulder strap on the case is very handy for travel. Make sure that the case is of sturdy construction to protect your valuable investment.

THE VIOLIN'S PLACE

13 PLACING OF THE VIOLIN IS IMPORTANT

The violin should be comfortably positioned, basically following the direction of your shoulder. Avoid neck strain caused by letting the violin drift too far off the shoulder and down onto the chest. The violin should be level from the scroll to the tailpiece, neither pointing down towards the floor nor up towards the ceiling.

14 PRACTICE A STRONG CHIN GRIP USING NO HANDS

The violin should be snug under the chin to allow more freedom for the left hand. Comfortable shoulder pads and chin pads can help you hold the violin better.

Practice tip: *"20-SECOND CHIN GRIP"*

Practice holding the violin with no hands for 20 seconds. Push the violin back into place if it starts to slip and try again. Increase the time, building up to a nice firm violin hold.

15 PROPER MAINTENANCE = BETTER SOUND

For good sound projection keep the violin clean. Excessive dirt and rosin buildup will clog up the sound and inhibit the wood's natural resonance. Keep the bridge upright and straight so it does not warp. The bridge is not glued on but is held in place by the tension of the strings.

Always keep the bow hair clean and avoid touching it with dirty fingers. To maintain a nice grip with the bow, keep the bow rosined and equipped with a full set of clean horse hair. Greasy bow hair will not grip the string. Check to see that the sound post is in its place so that the body of the violin will not collapse.

16 BE WISE ABOUT WHAT'S IN YOUR HANDS

Learn about all the **parts** of your instrument and your bow. Understand how they all function. This basic knowledge will help you take care of your investment properly.

Find the strings that give you the best sound. Cheap strings break easily and will not offer the desirable tonal quality.

Remember to loosen the bow after each use. Neglecting to do this will result in bow warping and having to replace the bow. The bow hair should not be so tight that it can't flex on the string while playing. Rosin improves the bow hair's ability to grip the string; conversely, no rosin means no sound. Refrain from tapping or hitting the music stand with your bow. The bow is fragile and can break easily, so be careful not to drop it.

POSTURE IS OF UTMOST IMPORTANCE

17 LAZY POSTURE = LAZY PLAYING

Stand as naturally as possible without slouching. Good posture will encourage clean playing. Stand up straight and tall, as comfortable and relaxed as possible. Do not contort your body into strange positions. Lazy posture can cause back and muscle strain.

18 COMMAND YOUR AUDIENCE'S ATTENTION

You don't want to appear sloppy or uninteresting, so look professional, standing tall and straight. Draw the attention of the listener to your music. Notice other performers' standing positions and mold your posture to the most desired position.

19 PRACTICE WITH THE MUSIC STAND AT THE PROPER HEIGHT

Purchase a music stand for your practice sessions. Adjust it to a height that will encourage good posture. If the music stand is at a low level, you will have a tendency to slouch over while practicing. You'll want to practice in comfort so that you are able to practice longer.

20 DON'T WASTE ENERGY

Save your energy for dynamic playing. Don't raise your shoulders as you begin to play. Let your shoulders hang. If your body is relaxed, you will not get as tired and you'll be able to perform longer. If you find that your arms or any other parts of your body are sore, check to see if you are wasting energy on too tight a grip of the violin or the bow.

21 THE MIRROR REVEALS PROBLEMS – TAKE A LOOK!

Find a mirror and see how you're doing. Are you holding the violin properly? Are you holding the bow properly? Is the bow placed on the strings in the right location? Is your bow straight? Are your fingers on the bow relaxed? Are your fingers on the violin straight and tall? Do you have an exemplary standing position? Practice in front of a mirror.

CHECKLIST:

- POSTURE
- VIOLIN HOLD
- FINGERS TALL ON FINGERBOARD
- BOW HOLD
- BOW PLACEMENT

22 BREATHE DEEPLY FOR SMOOTH PLAYING

Full breathing allows the brain to receive proper amounts of oxygen and lets the performer relax the body while playing. If you find that you are gasping for air at the end of a tune, then you are playing with too much tension somewhere in your body. Keep a relaxed chest cavity.

TUNING

23 FINE TUNERS MAKE TUNING EASY

When tuning, pull the bow across the strings slowly to hear the pitch; pulling too quickly can distort the pitch. Slowly loosen the peg and turn the peg tighter to raise the pitch (sharper), or looser to lower the pitch (flatter) and firmly push the peg into the peg box. Loosening the pegs first allows for ease in turning them. Remember to push the pegs in while you tune!

Fine tuners facilitate the tuning process.

24 PRACTICE TUNING OFTEN FOR PRECISION IN QUICK TUNING

Use your ears, listening very carefully to the pitch. Don't just wait for your teacher to give approval of the violin's tuning. Instead, listen and judge for yourself if the strings need adjusting. The more you tune, the easier it will become.

Avoid exposing your instrument to extreme temperature changes. Strings will change with weather changes. Major problems with the violin staying in tune could mean serious problems with the instrument. Ask a repair shop for an evaluation.

MASTER THE BOW

25 BOW FINGERS MUST BE SOFT AND RELAXED

Make sure that the thumb on the bow is tucked underneath and pointing up toward the middle finger. The fingers stay together "as a family" hanging over the bow and are not poised on their tips. Each finger should fall over the bow as your fingers do when the hand is relaxed and hanging by the side of the body. The pinky gets to ride up on top. Don't clench the bow, but keep gentle fingers on it. The fingers are along for the ride to maintain balance. Your stroke should be graceful and gentle. Approach the string with elegance. Hard, abrasive sounds are not pleasing to the ear.

The key to an excellent bow hand is a soft, relaxed hand with the fingers staying in their natural positions and not stretching apart.

26 KEEP YOUR FINGERS AND WRIST FLEXIBLE TO FACILITATE ADVANCED BOWING TECHNIQUES

It's time to "oil up" the wrist and the fingers on the bow. Loose, fluid movements are ideal for flexibility. Practice pushing the wrist up high on the up stroke and letting the wrist sink down on the down stroke. This releases tension in the wrist. The fingers should always rest softly on the bow, and feel flexible at the beginnings and ends of the bow strokes. This flexibility in the wrist and fingers is important for advanced bowing techniques.

27 KEEP A STRAIGHT BOW FOR A CLEAN SOUND

Straighten it up! Many players think that their bows are straight when their strokes are actually crooked. When bowing, open up and straighten the arm without pushing the elbow out and hitting the person next to you. There is a tendency to pull the frog of the bow towards your body. At the end of the stroke, push the frog away from the body and follow through with a straight bow.

Practice tip: *"QUIET BEGINNINGS AND ENDINGS"*

Place the bow on the string without making a sound. Pull out a nice long tone, finishing your bow stroke with no sound. Careful bowing will help form a style of clean playing, eliminating unwanted sounds.

28 USE ALL PARTS OF THE BOW

Don't get stuck at the tip or the frog. Advanced players are able to use all parts of the bow skillfully. The lower half of the bow will produce a heavier sound and the tip will give a lighter sound. Music changes from heavy to light, so you must be able to make these changes. Practice using proper bow distribution in your playing.

Practice tip: *"KISS THE FROG" or "KISS THE TIP"*

A great exercise for attaining a long bow is to practice playing all long notes ending at the tip and frog of the bow. Go farther on your stroke and "kiss the frog" or "kiss the tip".

29 FIND THE "SWEET SPOT" OF THE BOW

The sweet spot of the bow is the area that produces the richest sound. Playing at the frog will produce a heavy sound while playing at the tip will produce a lighter sound. Somewhere in the middle is a nice "sweet spot" where the bow is balanced between the heavy and the soft. Try to make every part of the bow a "sweet spot."

TONE

30 PRACTICE LONG, SLOW, SUSTAINED NOTES FOR EXCELLENT TONE

One of your goals on the violin should be to attain a beautiful sound. Ask yourself, "Was that bow stroke as pretty as I can possibly play it?" Practicing long, sweet bow strokes is advantageous for working on tone. Release pressure on the string if the sound is too harsh or scratchy.

Practice tip: *"THE 20-SECOND BOW RIDE FOR EXCELLENT TONE"*

Play long strokes on any scale and hold each note for twenty seconds. Twenty seconds will seem like a very long time, but patience during this exercise can promote better tone and bow control.

31 LISTEN CAREFULLY FOR A BEAUTIFUL TONE

"Are you listening carefully?" Many times you think you are listening, but you are not listening in a concentrated way. The closer you listen and are aware of extraneous sounds, the better you will be at cleaning up the sound. Are there any scratches or bumps? Aim for a smooth quality and beautiful sound. Pull into the string for the entire stroke with a straight bow. The weight of your arm should fall into the string.

BOW STRENGTHS

32 KEEP THE WEIGHT OF THE BOW AND THE ARM "IN" THE STRING

Fill the room with sound. Don't skim across the strings, but rather pull into the string. Don't press your fingers harshly on the bow. The fingers should merely help guide it without force.

33 PLACING THE BOW NEAR THE BRIDGE

Locate the placement of the bow on the strings that will offer the best sound. Near the bridge there will be a stronger, fuller sound and away from the bridge will give a softer, gentler sound. However, if you are too close to the bridge, the sound will be too harsh. If you play too far from the bridge, the strings are closer together and the playing gets a little sloppier. Find the lane that has the best sound. Playing over the fingerboard will not give you the clean, rich sound that you are want.

34 USING SOFTER TO HARDER BOW PRESSURE

Be conscious of the type of bow pressure that you choose to use in your music. Remind yourself to either pull a little more firmly or lighten up your stroke for the most appropriate sound. Practice experimenting with pulling the bow firmly only at the beginning of the stroke. Practice with the weight applied during the whole stroke. Practice with the weight at the end of the stroke. The goal is to increase your skill level to be able to use your bow in any fashion. Experiment making wave sounds with an open string for the softer to deeper tone.

Practice Tip: *"PIANISSIMO TO FORTISSIMO"*

Make your sound swell and increase in volume. Play an open string to the count of 15 seconds for an entire bow stroke, pulling and releasing the tension of the stroke. Notice the varied sound you can make with one stroke by releasing and adding pressure.

35 USING SLOWER TO FASTER BOW SPEED

The speed of the bow will alter the sound and intensity of the note. Experiment with different bow speeds. For the fullest sound use as much of the bow as possible, pulling the bow quickly across the strings.

Practice tip:
"10 to 5 to 1 to INCREASING
BOW CONTROL"

Play a full bow stroke to the count of 10 seconds. Then try the whole bow stroke to the count of 5 seconds increasing the bow speed to a 1-second bow stroke. This is an excellent exercise for bow control.

36 BOW LENGTH FOR AN AGGRESSIVE, FULL SOUND

Using a full bow, with the bow hair flat on the string and a pushing bow stroke, will produce a full sound. The longer the bow stroke, the louder the sound. Pull into the string with the weight of the bow and the arm. Many of the best players spare little of their bow when playing. Use the bow as the style you are playing requires.

37 FIND EXTRA MUSIC FOR BOW EXERCISES

If you want to develop a strong bow arm, you should practice supplemental bow exercises that require concentrated study. Seek out music books that focus on bow exercises and bow control. Keep working the frog, the middle and the tip of the bow. It is very beneficial to play a single etude using all of the common bowing patterns.

For example: First, play the etude with all separate bows; then, play the etude with slurs, all up bows, all stacatto, etc.

Practice tip: *"FROG TIME AND TIP TIME"*

Play an entire tune at the frog only. Next try playing only at the tip. Keep your drills interesting and challenging.

FAITHFUL FINGERS

38 FINGERS MUST STAND UP TALL ON THE FINGERBOARD

At first, learn with fingerboard tapes and watch to make sure that your fingers land precisely on the tapes. For beginners, the tapes on the violin fingerboard will help ensure hitting the right pitch. Once the correct hand position has been formed, the tapes can be removed. The fingers must stand tall and clean on the fingerboard.

NO LAZY FINGERS. A clean hand position will not allow lazy fingers to lie on the other strings.

Clip those fingernails short enough that your fingers can stand on their tips. Don't forget to learn the names of the notes you are playing. Instead of saying A1 or D3, use the proper note names.

Practice tip: **"NAME THAT NOTE"**

What is first finger on the A string called? What is first finger on the D string called? Go through the note names and be familiar with the A to G musical alphabet on your fingerboard.

Scales are one of the best exercises for your fingers. Be sure that your fingers are accurately hitting their positions.

39 PULL THE WRIST AWAY FROM THE NECK OF THE VIOLIN

Do not let the wrist crowd the hand by allowing the wrist to touch the violin. Pull the wrist out and away from the neck of the violin, making it easy for the fingers to stand tall and be placed cleanly on the fingerboard. Again, the hand must be as relaxed as possible.

40 THINK IN FINGER PATTERNS

When starting a composition consider the pattern that the fingers will form to. Each different key signature will have different patterns. Knowing these formations will help the ability of the violinist.

Will the fingers be close together or separated?

W W H W W W H

The major scale is made up of a whole step (W), whole step, half step (H), whole step, whole step, whole step and a half step pattern.

Remember to look at the key signature before playing for the correct positioning of the fingers.

41 TAP, TAP, TAP THOSE FINGERS FIRMLY

Your fingers should be strong and hit like little hammers on the fingerboard. If you barely press the string down, you will not produce a clear sound. Practice finger exercises for strength.

Practice tip: *"FINGER POPS"*

You can use any finger combination to practice popping the fingers down swiftly and firmly.

E1, E1, E1, E1, E2, E2, E2, E2, E3, etc.
1,2,3,4, 1,2,3,4, 1,2,3,4,
 4,3,2,1, 4,3,2,1, 4,3,2,1, etc.

42 SCALES ARE THE BEST!

Playing scales helps form proper hand positions. They will help you build note upon note to learn common finger patterns. Scales also help develop more precise **intonation**. If you have problems playing notes in tune, work on your scales and listen to each pitch carefully. Studying scales can give you a better understanding of music theory and build strength on the fingerboard.

Practice tip: *"CHROMATIC STEPS"*

Start on open A, progressing in half steps with a low 1, to 1, low 2, to 2, 3, to a high 3, 4th finger, etc. until you reach the next A an octave higher. Play this chromatic pattern over and over, slowly and carefully until you can play it easily. Next, try playing it backwards and then applying the entire pattern to each string.

43 INTONATION CLEAN-UP WITH PITCHES FROM THE PIANO

Playing along pitch by pitch with the piano is an excellent way to improve intonation. If you practice playing slowly with the piano – note by note and listening very carefully – your intonation will improve dramatically. Soon after the hand has formed its exact playing position and memorized where each pitch is, the tapes that were used for additional guides can be removed. You can also play along with recordings, first tuning your violin with an appropriate pitch.

RACING FINGERS

44 DON'T LIFT YOUR FINGERS FROM THE FINGERBOARD UNNECESSARILY

Keeping fingers down helps maintain the correct hand form and results in less wasted effort. If the fingers are already in their places, you will save time and energy as you won't need to relocate the fingers to their spots.

For faster passages, train your fingers to stay down until needed.

45 TIME YOURSELF TO IMPROVE YOUR SPEED

For the slower player, give your fingers a challenge: If you play a melody in 50 seconds, try to play it in 40 seconds, and get those fingers racing! Time yourself only on tunes that you have perfected, since playing too fast on new songs will only invite disaster. A metronome is also helpful for setting a faster tempo.

Practice tip: *"TIMING CHALLENGE"*

Time yourself on any tune in your repertoire and then play it faster.

EYES

46 EYES ON THE LOOKOUT!

Your eyes can watch over many things simutaneously. Look down the fingerboard and watch the precision of your fingers, tapping firmly. Watch the length of the bow, the location of your bow and how straight the bow is gliding across the strings. Your eyes can observe your standing position and the placement of your feet. Watch out for the proper placement of the violin on the shoulder, looking also in the mirror to ensure a beautiful playing posture.

Remember that in an orchestra, your eyes will need to watch the conductor as well as the music.

FEET

47 COMFORTABLE FEET AID COMFORTABLE PLAYING

Place your feet about a step apart. Generally, the left foot is placed under the elbow of the left arm; stiffly placing the feet will add tension, however, so be careful to feel comfortable when standing. Find a center of balance and refrain from placing all your weight towards one side.

48 PLACE YOURSELF IN AN ATMOSPHERE OF MUSIC AND LEARNING

If you want to grow in learning music then you need to be where the music is. Go to concerts, festivals, shows, workshops, classes or jamming sessions. Hang around those talented individuals in your life and learn all you can from them. You will even benefit from just listening to them play. Make your environment a place of music and learning.

PROPER PRACTICE

49 QUICKLY RUNNING THROUGH MUSIC = SLOPPY PLAYING

Some of the most beneficial practice is slow and careful practice. If you quickly run through a new song, then you will hit bumps and stumble. The brain needs time to process new data and log it in precisely. Once you can play a song smoothly and flawlessly at a substandard speed, then you can begin working up the tempo.

50 REVIEW IS SUPERB!
"Not the same old song, again!"

Remember that some of your best playing will come from the old pieces that you've played for years. ALWAYS, ALWAYS, ALWAYS review old tunes. This will strengthen your playing and add to your repertoire. Once you stop playing a tune it will easily slip from memory along with the skills required to play it.

51 SIGHT-READING IMPROVES YOUR READING ABILITIES

Practice sight-reading and read as much music as you can. What should you sight-read? Anything that you have available to you. Orchestra participation is very good for advancing in music reading.

52 UNDERSTANDING OF THEORY IMPROVES WITH INSTRUCTIONAL BOOKS

Your music theory knowledge will increase as you go through instructional books and continue reading music. There are music theory books that will explain every detail of the music staff and its components. Read all the fine print as you study these books so that you will learn what every marking means. Learn all note values, the different rests and their values, down bows, up bows, slurs, sharps, flats, accidentals, whole steps, half steps, chords, ties, intervals, etc.

Check out your local colleges for any music theory classes that they might offer.

53 CONTINUE LEARNING NEW TUNES

You should always be seeking out new pieces to learn. Pushing forward means studying, perfecting, and digesting as many pieces as possible. New tunes should be practiced slowly and carefully. You must precisely execute the correct finger and bow motion. When studying a new song, practice the scale of the song that you are learning. This will help you with the finger patterns.

54 MASTER A NEW SONG AND THEN PERFORM IT

When learning a new song you should have an incentive to work the song up to perfection. If you know that you will be performing a song for an audience then you will exert twice as much effort towards learning the song. Set performance dates for yourself so that you will strive towards a polished piece. Remember not to be in a rush when first learning a new song. Go step by step. Learn the first 4 measures, then the next 4 measures, and so on (section by section and then piece by piece).

Don't settle for the tune sounding just okay. Work on it over and over until it is polished. Sometimes, however, you reach a "wall" with a song where you don't seem to be making any progress. Remember to break the song down into small sections; work slowly, allowing time for your playing to season. There is a saying that goes, "An amateur practices a song until he can play it right. A professional practices until he can't play it wrong."

55 PROPER PRACTICE = PROGRESS

Slowly and carefully learn new songs. Review songs over and over to perfect your playing. Continue to sight-read new material. Read and learn music theory through instructional books. Master tunes section by section and finally perform beautiful music! Correct, thoughtful practice will enhance your performance.

CONCENTRATE

56 FOCUS AND BE ATTENTIVE

Be alert while you are playing. If you are attentive, you will be more aware of mistakes and bad habits that you might be forming. Keep your practice times reasonable so as to keep your mind alert and fresh. When practicing for an extended period of time, remember to take periodic breaks to insure an optimum practice session. A sleepy mind leads to mistakes.

NEW MUSIC

57 LEARN ALL THE MUSIC YOU CAN

Be a sponge for music and **soak it up!** Continue to try new material such as jigs, hymns, reels, concertos, hoedowns and classical, and popular selections. Try playing duet, trio and ensemble music. Exchange music with friends too.

58 LIBRARIES OFFER MORE

Many libraries offer the free loan of music books, CD's, tapes, and videos. Go see what's available!

Expand your skills; try classical, inspirational, contemporary, fiddle, jazz, sacred, blues, Irish, and Scottish music.

Begin to build your own music library. Start collecting piece by piece. Establish music categories so you can easily locate a given tune. Place music that is in a series in large binders for quick access.

HOW MUCH SHOULD I PRACTICE?

59 PRACTICE DAILY

A famous teacher once said to practice 2 to 3 times a day, but to break up the practice into half hour segments. Set a regular practice time and stick to it.

60 FREQUENT PRACTICE WILL SPEED YOUR LEARNING

The more often you play, the better you can become. Play music with family and friends, in school and church — everywhere, every chance you get.

Take 15 minute segments to run through the selection you are currently learning. Then put your instrument down, returning a little later to run through the music again. This type of frequent practice is better than putting in an hour of practice once a week.

61 LEARN TO LOVE PRACTICING!

Learn to enjoy your practice time, cultivating an eagerness to try a new piece or perfect that difficult passage. A positive attitude towards practice will encourage more learning.

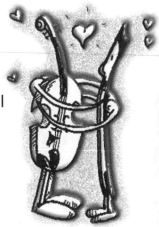

Practice tip: "*THE DOWN BOW and PLUCK GAME*"

Have fun and play a whole piece in down bows, plucking an open string (with the left hand) after each stroke.

LISTEN

LET YOUR EARS ENHANCE YOUR PLAYING

62 LISTEN TO MUSIC HOUR UPON HOUR

Every day, listen to music.

Always have beautiful music playing. This is an easy way to improve your skills. Those that listen to the songs that they are attempting to play learn faster than those who don't take advantage of listening. Listening is a shortcut to faster learning!

63 LISTEN TO MANY PERFORMERS

Each performer has his or her own unique characteristics, style, and strong points.

- Listen for phrasing and rhythms.

- Listen for style and tone.

- Listen for vibrato.

- Listen for major, minor, and blues patterns.

- Listen for all the colors.

64 LISTEN TO MANY STYLES

Listening to more styles can help your playing blossom, making you more versatile and creative. Listen for moods and details. Listen and learn from others. This is how you can grow in your playing!

65 RECORD YOUR MUSIC

You might be surprised at how you sound when you record yourself. I encourage you to casually record your practice. Later on, sit back and listen to what you actually sound like. Did you hear varied dynamics, scratches, or quality tone? You will hear your mistakes more clearly and can actively pursue making changes towards better playing if you are able to step back and listen.

MARKING MUSIC

66 DISSECT THE MUSIC, OBSERVING ALL THE MARKINGS

When studying a new piece of music, you need to know the meaning of all the musical markings on the page.

Define all the terms on your music with the help of a music dictionary. Figure out the key signature and time signature. Take notice of the metronomic markings and any accidentals. Don't just ignore the markings on your music; make an effort to find out what they mean.

Dissect and analyze the music until you know and understand every marking on the page. In pencil, write in the meaning of all the musical terms.

For example: Allegro — fast, grasioso — graceful, arco — with the bow, legato — smooth.

Watch for bow markings, fingerings, and other musical signs. When there are many markings present, slow practice is very beneficial.

67 ADD EXPRESSION MARKS TO YOUR MUSIC

The terms written on the music indicate to the performer what tempo, type of stroke, mood or sound the composer wanted to convey. Mark your music with written indications on how to expressively play the various sections.

For example: *attack, make it dance, louder, excited, waltz sound, brilliant, forceful, gentle, smooth,* etc.

Make extra notations for those accidentals you keep missing or might miss. Circle the accidental so that you notice it.

68 HIGHLIGHT WITH MAP PENCILS AND THEN COLOR YOUR PLAYING

Keep map pencils handy to highlight your music when practicing. Different dynamics should be shaded in different colors. Example: Forte = big & loud [shade it red]. Mezzo = medium [shade it orange], Piano = soft [shade it yellow]. Circle key changes in blue. Consider highlighting musical themes that keep repeating so that when you look at the music you will automatically see its structure (A A B C A). This will help in memorizing it.

Mark the different shades and tones, bringing color to your music paper so you can then *COLOR YOUR PLAYING!*

69 MAKE YOUR MUSIC DANCE AND SING!

After you have marked your music, you will need to enact all of that expressiveness. Music is more than written strokes on paper. It must turn into a song, taking away the robotic, stiff movements. Step away from your sheet music and make your music sing and dance by letting your heart take over.

70 THE MORE YOU MEMORIZE, THE MORE YOU *CAN* MEMORIZE

The mind, if trained properly, can grow in its capacity to memorize. Those brought up memorizing seem to be able to memorize more and more. Start small, memorizing a short song. To progress in memorizing a song, start with just a few measures at a time, building line upon line until you have completed memorizing the whole song. If you were to analyze the song, you would see repeated phrases. Breaking the song into parts, such as part A, part B and part C and then back to part A, will also help you in memorizing the song.

Listening to the song OVER and OVER and OVER again will greatly help in the memorizing process. Accurate memorization comes with repetitive listening!

71 ADD DAZZLING DYNAMICS

Bring your music to life with logical loud forte sections followed by soft piano parts. All music needs moving and changing color. You may think your music gets louder and softer, but in order for the audience to hear these changes, you must make them quite dramatically.

Create some fire, sizzle and tears in your playing. After your music is highlighted, you then need to incorporate the pencilled expressiveness into your playing. Writing "forte-loud"and actually playing loudly are two separate events. Ask someone to listen to see if they can indeed hear your dynamic changes. Record yourself to evaluate your dynamics to hear if they truly dazzle and sizzle. You may think that you are playing long bows or with great excitement and fire, but in listening to the recording, you might realize that your louds are not really that loud, your softs aren't all that soft, and there are very few color or dynamic changes in your music. Does your music evoke emotions strong enough to move your audience to tears?

72 TAKE ONE STEP AT A TIME AS EACH NOTE IS IMPORTANT

When studying a piece of music, it is best to take small steps. If you were to eat a steak, you would not swallow the entire piece of meat whole. You would take one manageable bite and thoroughly chew it before taking another. The same is true with a piece of music. If you attempt to study and memorize two new pages of music at once, you might choke on them. Take a few phrases at a time, perfecting, memorizing and then adding more. Remember, don't let even one note go by without making it sing.

73 MASTER THOSE DIFFICULT PASSAGES

Perfect all difficult passages and memorize them. How? Play the section at least 20 times. Most students run through hard sections only once or twice. Break down the hard section and play it repeatedly. It might take 50 times or 100 times, but then you'll have it! The best players execute difficult sections with ease as the result of their diligence in practice.

74 KNOW THE COMPOSER AND THE STYLE

Each composer displays his own style and purpose in his music. It is facinating to read about composers' lives and the events that inspired the music they wrote. Some music was written for dancing while other selections were intended for worship and singing or for specific instruments.

Bach, for example, wrote his music for the church. Routinely he wrote the abbreviation "S. D. G." (Soli Deo Gloria) on his manuscripts meaning *To God alone be the glory.*

Listen to recordings of various pieces written by the same composer, becoming familiar with the style and expressive techniques.

PERFORMING

75 ADD SPIRIT AND ENERGY

Is your performance energetic and dynamic? Make your music look fun and easy. The last thing anyone wants to do is sit around listening to boring perfor-mances. When you perform, be warm and personable to your audience, offering them energy and excitement in your playing.

76 MAKE A WHOLE-HEARTED EFFORT

Dress to perform and shine! You want to play at your highest potential, so look good and sound good. Diligent practice before performances is a must. Don't just barely pull it off, but offer all your energies and a whole-hearted effort. Ultimately music should come from the heart.

77 PLAY EFFORTLESSLY

Strive to get to a point where you can **play effortlessly**. Practicing a piece just a few times will not help you achieve this goal. Find a performance venue where you can continue to play those familiar songs dozens of times. The old tunes that you have played for years will be some of your best and will flow with ease.

78 NO BUMPS

If there always seem to be a couple of bumps in the music, then locate the problem areas first. Next, practice only these sections over and over until you iron out the problem. Slowly add those problem sections back into the piece, eventually playing the entire song without hesitation. What a great feeling to have mastered a difficult section in a challenging piece! Strive for the best in your playing, aiming to play with no mistakes and **no bumps**.

79 CONFIDENCE = STRENGTH IN PLAYING "WHERE CAN I FIND SOME CONFIDENCE?"

It's now time to play "in front of everyone" at every opportunity. Play for picnics, parks, nursing homes, family gatherings, neighbors, churches, youth clubs – *anywhere!* The more you play in public, the more comfortable you will become. Confidence will come as others tell you about the joy they experience in hearing your music.

CONFIDENCE = POWERFUL PLAYING.

80 MUSIC CAMPS AND INSTITUTES

Go to music camps and workshops. The intensified study and focus will propel your playing forward. Learn all that you can from everyone that you can. Check with the local colleges, libraries, city offices, or online sites for news of special educational opportunities.

81 COMPETITONS AND CONTESTS FOR EXCELLING

Entering competitions is an excellent means of pushing yourself to buckle down and perfect your music. These events should be looked on as another way to advance your playing. Sitting back at home with nothing to aim for will not inspire you to practice. The more competitions, challenges, all-city orchestras and tryouts you enroll in, the more you will be challenged to grow. Go for it!

82 REGULAR SOLO PLAYING IS A MUST!

If you play solos once or twice a year, how can you ever become a confident solo player? Fear can tear a lovely piece into shreds. Ideally, playing once a week in front of others would be wonderful. Even once a month is better than once a year. Start making arrangements for regular performances so that your confidence as a performer grows.

83 VIDEOTAPE YOURSELF

Videotaping your performances is extremely beneficial. You may find yourself thinking "Is that what I looked like? I thought that I was standing tall, looking professional and exciting. Is that what I really sounded like? I thought that I was using more of my bow and that I was playing louder." Evaluate your own playing, enhancing the good elements to become even better.

RELAXED PLAYING

84 NO TENSION

Calm down – aim for peace within your heart. Fear is a big enemy of relaxation and smooth playing. Think about keeping a loose body — even try to laugh a little to loosen up. Be focused on your strengths while enjoying the beautiful notes that you produce. While playing for others, don't dwell on mistakes or bumps; rather, look for enjoyment in upcoming passages.

85 TAKE A FEW STEPS

When performing, the body can tighten up and the legs can lock. Relaxing your legs, even taking a few steps while performing, will prevent leg-locking. Practice this at home, moving around the room to check for any stiffening of the legs.

Practice tip: *"WALKING SONG"*

When practicing your performance piece, walk from one part of the room to another.

86 SMILING

Tension can also accumulate in the mouth area. Don't lock your jaw or purse your lips while you are playing. If you open your mouth or smile occasionally, you will break the tension. If you *look* like you are enjoying your music, your audience will enjoy it much more. Your emotions and expressions will be perceived by your audience.
SHOW YOUR DELIGHT IN LEARNING AND PERFORMING.

87 HAVE SOME FUN, TOO!

Music should evoke emotion in your soul. Let joy project from your instrument. Enjoy your violin, allowing it to be a delight instead of a rigid chore.

Be quick to compliment and encourage others in their skill and accomplishments. "I really liked the song you played. Your long bows and vibrato were very pretty." Although it shouldn't be your motivation as you commend others on their performances, you too will begin to receive some positive feedback on your playing. This will propel you forward with the desire to perform more often.

If practice becomes boring, then consider changing your routine. There is time for work, but leave some time for play. Today, practice in your reading book and prepare for your solo repertoire, but also try playing that tune you heard yesterday. Find some new challenges for yourself and be creative.

88 FIND NEW CHALLENGES AND EXPERIMENT

Find out exactly what sounds your violin can make. Have a little fun trying some different sounds such as siren sounds, bird calls, a cat's meow, train sounds, slides, double stops & various rhythms.

See what that instrument can do. Play a melody in different keys or on different strings. Play a tune, adding open E or a plucked tone after each note. Games on the violin can be fun and helpful for increasing skill. Try playing all the melody notes twice, or even four times. Play the song with trills, tremolo, or in third position. Don't be afraid of your instrument, and learn something new today.

89 KNOW AND PLAY WELL-KNOWN EXCERPTS

There are many familiar tunes that almost everyone knows and loves. Learn these popular melodies and figure out how to play an excerpt from them. For example: 1) Our country's patriotic songs — Oh Say Can You See, Yankee Doodle; 2) orchestral compositions and opera themes — Beethoven's Fifth, the Four Seasons and Carmen; 3) popular TV and movie themes — Star Wars, Jeopardy and the Lone Ranger theme song; 4) hymns — Amazing Grace and Great is Thy Faithfulness; and 5) other favorites — Cinderella and Peter Pan.

RHYTHM

90 GIVE 'EM A BEAT TO REMEMBER

Practice music in different time signatures, (meters), becoming comfortable in each. There is common time (4/4), half time or cut time (2/4), jigs (6/8, 9/8, 12/8), waltz time (3/4), and so on. When learning a new tune, examine the time signature. Would you count it 1,2,3, 1,2,3, or 1,2,1,2, or 1,2,3,4, 1,2,3,4? Feel the beat throughout the tune.

In an ensemble or band, listen very carefully to the lead instrument's rhythm. Some players get so caught up in their own playing that they don't listen to others. When there is no solid beat, the music is even more difficult to play. When playing

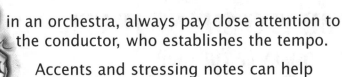

in an orchestra, always pay close attention to the conductor, who establishes the tempo.

Accents and stressing notes can help confirm the feel of the rhythm. When rhythm difficulties occur, work out the beats very slowly to find the main pulsations of the measure. Counting out loud or clapping the rhythms while focusing only on meter and rhythms can help iron out problem areas.

91 PRACTICE WITH A METRONOME

Metronomes are useful in setting the exact tempo for a piece and can help identify a timing or rushing problem.

If there is a particularly difficult problem with rhythm, try having some fun with a drum. Pop in a tape of the piece you are working on and beat out the rhythms. You must feel the beat inside of you, working with it until you feel smooth and comfortable with the rhythm. Can people clap with the beat of your playing? Can someone dance to your rhythm?

VIBRATO-SHAKE IT UP!

92 LOOSEN-UP THE GRIP

First, your left hand must be very relaxed. Practice a slow, wide movement with the knuckles waving towards your face and then back towards the scroll. The more tension and resistance in your hand, the less movement you will achieve. Continue practicing this slow wave motion (called vibrato) with each finger on each string gradually transitioning to a faster, tighter wave.

93 OFFER A VARIETY OF SPEEDS

Learn to play vibrato at various speeds. Try a whole note with a slow, wide vibrato. For a whole different effect, try an intense vibrato speed with each finger, not letting any of the fingers go down without the intense motion. Each song creates a unique mood and sound. Some songs have very intense sections that would call for a dynamic vibrato, while others may have a romantic nature and need a slower, gentler touch. Experiment with the various vibrato techniques for the optimum sound.

Practice making waves — a swelling effect — by pushing the knuckles forward and back. Next, start the long sustained note with a slow vibrato that increases in strength and intensity. Finish the stroke with a slower, wider, fade out vibrato.

Practice tip: *"EACH FINGER WAVES"*

Play a tune with full, long bows. Don't let a single note go by without applying vibrato to it.

SHIFTING

94 AIM FOR SMOOTH & SWEET SHIFTING

Make your shifting light, free, and easy. Loosen up your grip on the neck of the violin so your hand can move freely. Practice the shift over and over again until you feel comfortable with it. Sliding into and out of shifts instead of stiff leaps adds character and

aids in smooth shifting. Don't take the easy way out by escaping the shift and playing only in "first position".

THE MORE YOU SHIFT POSITIONS THE SWEETER IT WILL BECOME. Those who have more experience in shifting can shift with greater ease and confidence. Special instructional books with shifting exercises will help strengthen your shifts.

For the shift, the violin should be held firmly with the chin, allowing the fingers to move freely on the strings. The thumb should curve around and under the neck as the hand moves up. Release the weight of the finger and the bow before the shift. Repeat the shift over and over again. Concentrate on the feel of the shift.

Practice tip: "SHIFTING UP IS EASY"

Try playing the A scale on the A string using only the first finger. This can help loosen up the hand. Then try the second and third finger, going all the way up the scale on one string. Do this on each string with the appropriate scale.

Practice tip: *"ONE STRING ONLY"*

Attempt playing an entire song on one string as a shifting exercise.

95 FORTIFY YOUR PLAYING IN HIGHER POSITIONS WITH EASY, FAMILIAR SONGS

To gain command of higher positions, try playing easy songs in different positions. For example, play "Twinkle" in 2nd, 3rd, 4th, and 5th positions. This will facilitate easy shifting. Explore various hand positions on different strings. Practice playing a song like "Amazing Grace" in regular position and then up an octave. Advance to playing the song in a third octave. The three-octave scale practice will benefit you in many ways, freeing up your hand for advanced techniques.

Practice tip: *"THE 3-OCTAVE SONG"*

Play a simple song in three different octaves.

IMPROVISE

96 DON'T BE STUCK TO THE SHEET MUSIC: AD LIB

It's now time to add-in your own music. Don't show up at a musical gathering to say that you can't play because you left your sheet music at home. Be creative and play from your heart.

Knowing the key signature and the scale of a piece is essential for improvisation. If the song is in G major, then practice the G major scale, learning the finger pattern and all the notes that are available for improvising in the song. Next, you will need to stay with the rhythm. Start with easy whole-notes and half-notes, then advance to varying eighth-note, quarter-note and sixteenth-note rhythms.

You can also begin to improvise by playing an easy familiar song to which you can add extra notes. Play in groups that will allow you to improvise, such as "jam sessions," or just put on a CD and have fun creating your own music to it.

97 USE A "BAG OF TRICKS"

When improvising it's important to apply a variety of ideas. Play the notes in the scale ascending, descending, and skipping. Play the arpeggios going up and down, using various octaves. Play octaves and chords. Try adding trills, grace notes and turns. Slide into and out of notes with sweet shifts.

Enhance your dynamics with louds and softs, fading into and out of phrases. The bow can add many new aspects to the music with slurs, staccatos, accents, and tremolo. Add harmonics, pizzacato, and double stops. Vary the rhythms of the notes with sixteenths, quarter-notes, half-notes and triplets. Don't always just play the melody, but change up and play the rhythm parts. Using this "bag of tricks" will help you create and improvise even better.

BE TEACHABLE

98 ASK OTHERS HOW YOU MIGHT IMPROVE

Be open to taking advice and learning. Ask for comments from others. Although it may be painful to hear some of your flaws, your desire to improve should far outweigh the fear of hearing about the weaknesses in your playing. In addition,  you will hear what others see as your strengths. Ask what you can do better and how you can improve.

99 BUILD UPON YOUR MISTAKES AND ENJOY YOUR ACCOMPLISHMENTS

Build upon your mistakes and don't quit. Take note of your weak areas and begin to practice those daily, strengthening your playing.

Find pleasure in your accomplishments and nourish the excitement of learning more. Remind yourself of the strong points in your playing and focus on highlighting them and making your overall playing exciting.

100 FIND AN INSPIRATIONAL TEACHER

Find a good teacher to coach you and encourage you to develop properly. Lessons are beneficial at any age. A teacher will hold you account-able and keep you studying and practicing weekly. During lessons, take notes so that you won't forget important points. Most of the great performers stud-ied with several teachers. Each teacher can offer different tools to help you progress. Learn all you can from each teacher and always remember to express your appreciation of them. When you thank your teachers for passing on their knowledge and gifts to you, they will be eager to share more with you.

101 APPLY YOUR MUSIC AS THE GREAT COMPOSERS DID

It is important to include biographies of composers in your home library. As you study a piece, read about the composer. This will give you insight into the style, the background, influences, and the impact these individuals had on the world.

Take note of some of the great composers and the purpose of their music:

Bach, aspired "to create well-regulated church music to the glory of God." He fathered twenty children and the fruit of his musical genius remains today. The final composition that Bach, completely blind, dictated from his bed was "Before Thy Throne I Come."

Beethoven, though deaf towards the end of his life — was a virtuoso pianist. His father was an alcoholic and his sickly mother died at the age of only forty. With hardship and great sadness in his life, he wrote in his diary, "In whatsoever it be, let me turn to Thee and become fruitful in good works". Beethoven left us many beautiful compositions to enjoy.

Handel, after writing the "Hallelujah Chorus," had tears streaming down his face and said, "I did think that I did see all Heaven before me, and the great God

Himself." When the King of England stood during the performance of the "Hallelujah Chorus", the entire audience also stood in accordance with royal protocol. To this day, audiences still rise to their feet during the performance of this magnificent composition.

These devoted composers created beautiful music for their God, king and country and generations to come.

MAY YOU BE BLESSED IN YOUR ENDEAVORS!!

Information provided on classical composers was derived from <u>The Spiritual Lives of Great Composers</u>, Patrick Kavanaugh, Nashville: Sparrow Press, 1992.

Would you like to hear Sandy and Clint Hunt:

Table for Two (CD only)
A contemporary inspirational album featuring original songs by Sandy and Clint Hunt is available from:
Forest Road Productions
P.O. Box 16123
Chesapeake, VA 23328

Please send you check or money order for $12.95 plus $3.95 (shipping) made out to Forest Road Productions. Thank you!

Fiddle Album (CD only)
Ask about the *Hunt Family Fiddle Album*. This exciting collection of jigs, reels, airs, and bluegrass tunes are a highlight from many performances of the Hunt Family Fiddlers. Available in Fall 2001 from:

Forest Road Productions
P.O. Box 16123
Chesapeake, VA 23328
www.huntfamilyfiddlers.com